Island hopp

The football grounds of…

by Steven Penny

First published in Great Britain in 2022

Penny For Your Sports Publications

ISBN: 978-0-9541392-8-5

Unless stated, pictures are by the author.

Cover photographs
Front – main image: Club La Santa *(courtesy of Club La Santa)*,
Logo of Lanzarote *(designed by Cesar Manrique, © Cabolt Lanzarote)*

Back – main image: Haría
Insets, from top left:
Tahíche, UD Lanzarote, Guatiza, Unión Sur Yaiza,
Sporting Tías and Puerto del Carmen

steve@stevepennymedia.co.uk

A Penny For Your Sports production

Contents

But why Lanzarote?

When I first announced I was writing a book about football on Lanzarote, I was met with looks of disbelief and questions as to how it would make more than a leaflet. I must admit, before flying to the Island of Eternal Spring, I also thought it was little more than a one-team 'town' with UD Lanzarote the only side I had vaguely heard of.

As a freelance journalist, I find it hard to relax – always looking for my next story or a new angle to keep paying those bills!

That does mean that on holiday I find it hard to relax and after a few days soaking up the sun, invariably find myself going off in search of a football game to watch – proper football mind, none of that TV boxed variety.

So, seeking some winter sun and 'knowing' – after looking on the excellent *uk.soccerway.com* website – there were only one or two grounds on Lanzarote and the chances of seeing any action was slim due to the timing of my flights, I thought I might be able to actually recharge my batteries. A sneaky bit of pre-trip research for lower levels revealed there might be a few more grounds on the island but barely worth lifting my no-doubt lobster-coloured body from the sunbed to investigate.

Oh, how wrong I was...

As far as I am aware – and I did look hard, believe me – there has never been a book about football on Lanzarote written in English. Hopefully, this publication fills that gap and will whet your appetite to try a taste of football, Lanzarote-style!

My immense gratitude goes to Antonio Brito, of the Altavista club, whose encyclopaedic knowledge of all things football on Lanzarote was incredible and his advice and the ability to rattle off answers to my Google Translate-assisted questions was a massive bonus. Thanks also to Ian Lane, at UD Lanzarote, who provided the answers to my initial questions, after bombarding him at all hours, being grateful to find someone on the island with a footballing knowledge who spoke English.

I also wish to thank Vicente Masia Pous, of the Spanish Football Encyclopedia; Augustine Hernandez, Sarabel and Chino, of the Web de Lanzarote; whose research I dipped into. I was unable to contact any of them but wish to place on record my thanks for their missionary work in digging up the island's incredible footballing history. Thanks also to all the individuals and clubs who replied to my requests, written in what must have seemed pidgin Spanish, for information and pictures. Credit also to the compilers of the many websites containing information about football on Lanzarote and in Spain generally. A more complete list of all those 'assistants' is at the end of this book.

Special thanks go to the Cabolt Lanzarote for giving me permission to use the Lanzarote 'Sun Volcano symbol' artwork, which was designed by Cesar Manrique.

I am also grateful to my son Jordan for his artistic skills in being able to pull together my scrappy drawings and bitmapped, low-resolution pictures of club badges and kits and transform them into something wonderful.

Any errors are mine. Please let me know of any you spot and they will be corrected in any reprints.

Steven Penny,
Suffolk, UK, July 2022

Let's go explore...

There's only so much sun, sea and sangria a man can take on a winter sunshine break to Lanzarote. While my wife caught up on her reading and trying to bring colour to her winter pallor, it seemed a suitable time for me to go exploring.

I set a target of visiting all 11 grounds hosting senior football on the island over the course of the week. However, Lanzarote is so small and easy to get around, I managed that in just three half days, picking up eight others I had not known about, including two abandoned ones, and learned about the only grass pitch on the island. As for actual live action, I watched three games, but could have added several more had I wished, thanks to a full programme of midweek floodlit action.

Less than 40 miles from north to south and about 16 miles at its widest point, my groundhopping adventure, which also included some additional non-football sight-seeing, cost less than £30 in fuel for my hire car.

Road trip: A car is the best way to explore the island

Lanzarote is home to 16 senior clubs, playing at 11 venues (17 and 12 after the summer elevation of Inter Play Honda), with another half-dozen-or-so clubs at junior and veteran levels, as well as a communal stadium in the capital Arrecife. Despite its small size, the Island of Eternal Spring boasts two clubs in the fifth level of the Spanish league system, four more in a Canary-wide competition as well as a league of its own. Thriving junior and youth leagues, women's competitions and a veterans league ensure there is always plenty of action to catch, with all grounds floodlit and boasting artificial pitches.

The roads are generally quiet and many are recently built, giving smooth access to most parts of the island. Beware though, many of the old roads remain and are popular with cyclists. Unfortunately, some are dead ends for cars, so expect a few U-turns if your sat-nav is not up to date! There are also lots of one-way systems in towns and villages and in many cases they all seem to go the same way, so it can be a real task trying to work out how to drive to the 'other end' of the street. Also, roundabouts can be a challenge. It is not so much that you have to think 'continental' giving way to the left in your left-hand drive vehicle, but many boast a tangle of exits – some marked on the sat-nav, many not and others being drive-ways, tracks or lay-bys. However, if you keep your wits about you, driving on Lanzarote really is a doddle.

Grey day: Lanzarote is not the most colourful of islands

If you do not fancy taking charge of your own destiny, however, the island has a good bus service. More than 30 routes are listed on the excellent website, covering most parts of the island, with a multitude in and around Arrecife and the main tourist areas of Puerto del Carmen and Costa Teguise. Unfortunately, apart from airport services, very few run after 10pm and weekends can be sporadic. The website has a comments board and queries are answered rapidly in English – *https://tinyurl.com/LanzaBus*

As well as a boost to your vitamin D levels with a guaranteed blast of sunshine, Lanzarote can be a home from home with English widely spoken in the main tourist areas. It is a volcanic island so don't expect lots of idyllic greenery. It is grey and dusty but most tourists venture no further than the bar from the beach and seem quite happy to occupy their stay in full relaxation mode. It is definitely a holiday isle, so there are flights all year round from most regional UK and European airports.

Forbidding walls: Campo de Fútbol Municipal de Argana

Canarywise, there are inter-island flights, as well as ferries to Gran Canaria and Tenerife.

Sitting 80 miles off the coast of Africa and 600 miles from the Spanish mainland, football on Lanzarote does tend to be parochial, although a couple of clubs have played as high as Segunda B. The neighbouring islands of Gran Canaria and Tenerife currently host Segunda League fixtures and CD Tenerife and UD Las Palmas do have La Liga pedigree, so progress is not impossible.

UD Lanzarote and Union Sur Yaiza are the highest-ranked clubs on the island, both playing in section 12 of the Tercera División. That season runs from September until May. Four more teams compete in the Preferente División – San Bartolomé, CD Tahiche, Sporting Tías and newly promoted Tinajo – one step down in a slightly shorter October-April campaign, with the remaining 11 teams playing in the Lanzarote regional division, which starts in November and runs to May.

It was fun and games tracking down some of the grounds. Many are similar, with high, white walls and often a grand entrance – but occasionally what I thought was the ground would be hiding a hotel, leisure centre or, next to CD Tite, what looked like a scrapyard.

Thankfully, floodlights, burst out of the barren earth, like futuristic lighthouses beckoning fans in, with the metal monsters getting ready to throw out their volcanic bolts of light to show emphatically where the real action is; not on a cosy settee or crammed together in a bar.

In my pursuit of ground pictures on non-match days, in many cases it was fingers crossed to find open gates. The artificial surfaces need minimal attention so they are often not opened up until shortly before kick-off. I was foiled only once – thankfully the Tahiche ground is overshadowed by a volcano, so I was able to clamber up to get an aerial view.

It was a tremendous vista but I'm not sure it was worth the grazes and abrasions I suffered as I skidded my way back down the pumice-like rocks. I struck lucky at a couple of grounds, which had looked impossible to get into, with my visits coinciding with the arrival or departure of kindly workmen who allowed me brief access.

Virtually all grounds offered deep terracing along one side, some with cover, some with plastic seats. Most were single-sided with limited or no access to the other three sides for spectators. All were well maintained, even one at Guatiza, which has a volcanic grit surface and is now only used by a 'veterano' team. I had discovered another ground nearby, which appeared to be virtually on the beach but, alas, the only trace of it now remaining is a solitary set of goalposts on Google Street View. That was also the case at Uga, where another grit ground still has its floodlights but no sign of the pitch. It is a similar situation in Arrecife, where the former home of SCRD Torrelavega has been left to rot with only the floodlight pylons and an expanse of bare ground to mark its position.

And so to some actual football. Friday evening brought the first taste with a trip east to see Club Deportivo Tinajo take on CD Orientación Marítima. That came via a roundabout route, taking in the stadiums at Puerto Del Carmen, Yaiza and San Bartolomé – the latter two are dwarfed by neighbouring volcanoes (think Frickley Athletic in the 1970s and 80s with the omnipresent slag heap!). Thankfully, although Lanzarote boasts more than 200 volcanoes, only one is active – Timanfaya, where the El Diablo restaurant offers meals cooked with volcanic heat.

Identikit: Many of Lanzarote's grounds have a similar layout

I arrived at Los Volcanes, the Campo de Fútbol Municipal de Tinajo home of Tinajo, for their match against Orientación Marítima. I was early and so followed players through the small access gate in the huge main gates. However, a lack of tracksuit and kit bag signalled me out as an imposter – not the 30-40 year age difference and T-shirt-stretching stomach I'm sure! I was ushered back outside to a small hatch, which was opened to relieve me of a 3€ entry fee. I was handed a ticket but this was quickly snatched off me back at the gate before I even had chance to say *gracias*.

The canteen and club shop already looked busy an hour before the 9pm kick-off. I took a place on concrete benching on the open seating and noticed a small room at the far end of pitch, with a fair bit of activity round it. Surprisingly, as well as every spectator and official wearing masks, the players were also warming up in similar face coverings. Suddenly the home players broke off from their preparations and headed to the mystery room. The door opened and the referee emerged with a gun!

There was no need to call the police thankfully. He was simply taking the players' temperatures as part of his pre-match checks. The away team had been busy in a meeting in their dug out, as access to the changing rooms was restricted by the Covid measures in place across Spain. They took their turn for temperatures checks, allowing the match officials time to do their own warm-up routine. No jogging up and down the pitch for this trio though, they got a ball and started spraying passes backwards and forward across the penalty area to each other.

Team talk: Outdoor pre-match chat at Tinajo for Orientación

I was surprised to see the match kick off with players and officials continuing to wear their Covid-protection masks. Although the referee and players had theirs under their chins, the assistants kept theirs over the mouths and nose throughout. Whenever the referee spoke to a player, both would pull up their masks to cover their face.

An attendance of about 200 people consisted of a large number of women and young couples, mainly supporting the home team in blue.

That game finished 2-1 to the home side and so it was on to Saturday and a step up the Lanzaroteños pyramid with Preferente Interinsular action at

Sporting Tías. It also gave me chance for a trip round the island to tick off the grounds of Tahiche, Guatiza, Haria and Teguise. The Campo de Fútbol Municipal de Tías is home to PDC Fútbol 2016, but it was landlords Sporting Tías who I was watching, welcoming Unión Deportiva Balos from Las Palmas.

My entry fee of 5€ was this time paid through a small window at the side of the entry gate but, again, the ticket was no sooner in my grasp than it was snatched away and torn in half. At least this time I got half as a souvenir!

A small shop was selling scarves, caps and pin badges, as well as refreshments, and a reasonable crowd was gathering. Again it was a fairly young and mixed-sex attendance, this time with a dozen or so teenagers with a big drum. The teams entered the arena up a walkway from beneath the long, covered stand, marching out to AC/DC's Highway to Hell, played by a DJ in the front of the fans. A first half of few chance brought little chance to cheer for the 300-or-so fans and it was not until the second half that things livened up, with the hosts earning a 2-0 win.

Sunday was the big one – Unión Deportiva Lanzarote at home to Villa Santa Brigida in the Tercera División at the island's biggest stadium by far. The Ciudad Deportiva ground is barely 100 yards from Arrecife bus station, so is popular with residents, holidaymakers and ex-pats alike. Built as an athletics stadium, fans are separated from the action by a six-lane track and a plethora of field hardware.

Today's noon kick-off attracted a crowd of about 350 and there was another arresting sight on arrival. A policeman was pointing a gun at fans – this time administering sanitiser on their hands, with a club official then directing another 'weapon' at their foreheads to take their temperatures.

I was there: Entry ticket from CDF Sporting Tías

Guarded welcome: Entry checks at UD Lanzarote

Entry was via a small trestle table holding a cash box and a lady taking the 8€ admission. Club souvenirs and refreshments were not available due to Covid restrictions but there is a club shop selling shirts and memorabilia in Costa Teguise, as well as an online one. Bizarrely, at this level, the usual ground sales are not allowed, but players can play without masks. Lower down the leagues, shops and refreshments are available but players and match officials must keep their masks on throughout the game. In all instances, masks must be, and are, worn, by the spectators, even in the open and when several yards away from the nearest other person. It is not just the UK that has had some baffling Covid rules.

The ground has a large covered stand with open seating either side and also at the scoreboard end of the ground. There is no access to the near side, where the club offices and changing rooms are located. Today's crowd included a small band of vocal home fans, mainly 30-50 year old men and a couple of women but with a few younger ones and boosted by the ranks of youngsters from match visitors Costa Teguise Juniors. With obligatory big drum and a couple of flags, waved less and less vigorously by a couple of middle-aged men as the game wore on, it did create a decent atmosphere.

Lanzarote are one of few teams on the islands to have regular away support and ex-pat Ian Lane, who runs an informative English website for the club – *https://mercancialanzarote.com* – said: "We arrange away trips to Fuerteventura with bus, boat and a roll and drink. Normally it costs only 20€. If you are a resident in the Canarian islands you get 75 per cent discounts on flights to anywhere in Spain. This means a return flight to Tenerife can be around 40€, so many residents organise themselves and make a weekend of it."

Today's vocal followers sang and chanted throughout, despite a fairly low-quality match, which was eventually decided by a second-half penalty in favour of the visitors, who also had a first-half spot kick saved. Most chants and songs were in Spanish, albeit with recognisable tunes in many cases.

Despite the heat, many of the home fans remained resplendent in not only their red, white and blue club shirts but also with woollen scarves around their necks.

The quiet Sunday city streets gave me the chance to visit the city's other grounds. As well as league stadiums at Altavista and CD Tite, there are junior level grounds at Playa Honda (since elevated back to the Lanzarote League), San Francisco Javier and Las Salinas, plus the shared Municipal Stadium, the abandoned Torrelavega ground and the training facilities of Marítima – another full-size pitch, albeit without spectator facilities.

The island's only grass pitch is at La Santa. The sport resort is currently only open to guests, due to Covid precautions, but has played host to some of Europe's top teams for warm weather preparation.

Lanzarote's final pitch, was one I did not get to as, technically, it is not on the island.

La Graciosa is the 'eighth' Canary Island but, as part of the Teguise council area, it does come under Lanzarote's jurisdiction.

Although the tiny island, off the north west coast, has no paved roads, it did boast its own football ground. That is long abandoned but, thanks to the wonder of the worldwide web and Google street view, there are pictures of what I missed.

Catch 'em young: Costa Teguise juniors at UD Lanzarote

The early days

It took several failed attempts before football finally gained a toe hold on Lanzarote. The Swedes were the first to try to introduce the sport to the island in 1903 when the crew of the Saga, which was passing the island, stopped off for a practice match.

However, it was another seven years before the first organised attempt at organised football on the island came, courtesy of a pair of brothers returning to Lanzarote from their studies in England. Antonio and Manuel Molina Orosa were the pioneers, introducing it to the island's youth. Sons of an Arrecife merchant, they formed two teams according to the colour of the clothes they wore – Los Blancos and Los Negros.

According to the archives of Agustín Hernández, reported on the *lafutbolteca.com* website, after this trial, the first club was created on the island – the Club de Gimnasia y Recreo de la Sociedad Democracia de Arrecife. Unfortunately, as soon as the Molina brothers returned to England to continue their studies, the fledgling sport ceased.

Picture: ©Agusti Hernandez

Los Negros: Lanzarote football 1910s style.

A third attempt came in 1916, following a boom in football on Gran Canaria and Tenerife, but the native Canarian wrestling, cricket and handball still remained more popular on Lanzarote.

It was not until 1924 that several clubs appeared in Arrecife – CD Arrecife and CD Lanzarote – with another being formed in Teguise – CD Guanapay.

The Camp Salinas (the Atlantic Stadium) was opened in July 26, 1925, with a match between Arrecife and Guanapay, followed by an inter-island clash against Las Palmas club

Real Club Victoria. Those early clubs failed to last but in 1930 Fénix emerged (funded by Sociedad Democracia), CD Culantrillo (funded by the Culantrillo Culture Society) as well as CD Teguise. These three clubs took part in a local competition, receiving a trophy donated by tailor Don Francisco Fábregas.

By 1935, Gimnástico, a new Lanzarote and Titerroy-Gatra had emerged but all sporting activity was interrupted by the Civil War soon after. During this period, football continued to be played against military teams, including German ship Scheleswig Holstein, whose crew beat a team of local players 11-0.

CD Teguise: One of the oldest surviving clubs, here in 1927

Remaining clubs were made up of soldiers stationed in Lanzarote, creating the Artillery and Infantry teams, to go with Haría, Jameos, Arrecife and Teguise.

At the end of the war in 1942, the Lanzarote Olympic Stadium was inaugurated, located on the grounds of Las Salinas with a 5,000 capacity, with a match between Teguise and Caimanes del Jameo 133.

Until 1943 the clubs continued to be of a military nature, among them CD Avión, the Leones 33 Battalion, Caimanes del Jameo 133, Guanche, Infantry and Artillery Tigers.

A local league was created in 1944 with teams including Osborne, Educación y Descanso, Marino, Torrelavega and another new CD Lanzarote.

Clubs came and went over the next few decades with a variety of league disputes and then heavy flooding around the Olympic Stadium curtailed the activities of Arrecife, Puntilla and Lomo in 1959. Agustín Hernández tried to organise a championship with Torrelavega, Estudiantes, Lanzarote and Lomo but it failed to prosper.

CD Juventud then came to prominence, along with a new club, CD Orientación Marítima, who began as a youth team and made rapid progress all the way to the national Second Division B. More clubs appeared, including San Fernando and Carmen, who later became part of Torrelavega and Lanzarote respectively.

In 1964 the island was visited by Antonio Avendaño Porrúa, the civil governor of Las Palmas, who decided to build a new stadium in Arrecife to meet the demands of higher level football. It was financed by José Antonio Elola Olaso with the department for Physical Education and Sport subsidising half of the work. In 1968 the Avendaño Porrúa Stadium was unveiled, just in time for the island to create its own 'superclub'.

Football and tourism were both making an impact on the island by the late 1960s and the idea was circulated of forming a powerful club to represent Lanzarote on the national Spanish stage. It had been shown that the various island communities could not do that on their own but the thought was that, jointly, they could. Thus Unión Deportiva Lanzarote was born in July 1970 , thanks to an agreement by clubs including Orientación Marítima, CD Lanzarote, Torrelavega, Valterra, Lomo, Arrecife and Teguise to give their best players to the new club. Based at the new Avendaño Porrúa Sports Complex, (later Sports City of Lanzarote) the new club joined the Second Provincial Regional League, rising to the First Regional League in 1973.

Picture: ©Agusti Hernandez

An Olympian effort: The island's former Olympic Stadium

Promotion to the Preferential Regional League followed in 1978, with a switch to the Canarian Third Division in 1980. The club eventually achieved its highest level, Segunda División B, in 1999 and spent 10 of the following 11 seasons just two levels below the Spanish elite, even winning the title in 2004 but missing out on promotion in the play-offs.

Meanwhile, a wave of interest had swept across the island and many more clubs became established with the island league thriving and providing promotion opportunities for ambitious clubs. Haria, Orientación Marítima, Teguise and Yaiza have all enjoyed spells in the Tercera División, with Orientación even managing a single season in Segunda B in 2006/7.

As a sidenote, it is not only football that has been played on some of the island's grounds. Cricket was also introduced by the English several years ago –playing on the volcanic granules that made up the pitches at that time. Coconut matting was laid across the centre circle to offer something like an even surface to bowl on.

Matches were first played at the Yaiza ground – the spiritual home of the sport on the island – and the introduction of artificial turf ensured a much smoother game for the cricketers.

Eventually a mini tri-league was created between Lanzarote CC, Playa Blanca CC and St George's CC, the three founder members of what was to become The Lanzarote Cricket Association. Games were also played at Puerto del Carmen and Tías and the island league increased to eight clubs, with an island representative team eventually formed, taking on touring teams arriving from England and Ireland.

Most game are now played at Puerto del Carmen's football stadium and the sport continues to thrive in this most unlikely of outposts.

Pictures: ©Agusti Hernandez

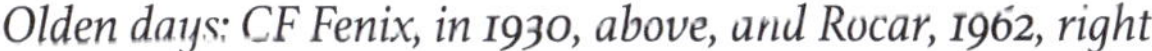

Olden days: CF Fenix, in 1930, above, and Rocar, 1962, right

How it works

The 2022/23 season will see 17 teams from Lanzarote competing across three levels of the Spanish football pyramid.

Alas, none will be at the highest level, La Liga, indeed no club from the island has ever played in those upper echelons of the game.

However, both UD Lanzarote and Orientación Marítima have played in Segunda B, then the third level, within fairly recent memory.

The Spanish football pyramid has a maximum of 10 steps following a reorganisation and the introduction of a new third tier in 2021/22.

Lanzarote has representatives at steps 5, 6 and 7 (Tercera División 12, Interinsular – Gran Canaria, Fuerteventura and Lanzarote – and a Lanzarote-only league). The lower regional divisions do not include the island.

Promotion and relegation over recent seasons has been complicated by the need for play-offs, ahead of the introduction of the new system, and also due to the coronavirus pandemic and the travel and match restrictions that brought.

It is now a straight series of play-offs between the top four at each level to determine which team will go up. At times, the Lanzarote League (level 7) winners have also faced a 'super' play-off with a two-legged tie against the winners of the Fuerteventura league.

The reorganisation caused some imbalances in the system and, remarkably, the 2021/22 season saw seven sides relegated from UD Lanzarote's 17-team Tercera División RFEF 12 – the island team finishing, thankfully, just above them.

The Spanish pyramid

Level 1: La Liga
2: Segunda División
3: Primera División RFEF (two groups)
4: Segunda División RFEF (five groups)
5: Tercera Divisions (18 groups)
6: First Regional Division (37 groups)
7: Second Regional Division (74 groups)
8: Third Regional Division (94 groups)
9: Fourth Regional Division (81 groups)
10: Fifth Regional Division (six groups)

Lanzarote teams 2022/23

Tercera (2): Lanzarote and Union Sur Yaiza.

Interinsular (4): San Bartolomé, Sporting Tías, Tahiche and Tinajo

Lanzarote League (11): Altavista, Arrecife, Haria, Inter Playa Honda, Lanzarote B, Orientación Marítima, PDC Fútbol 2016, Puerto del Carmen, San Bartolomé B, Teguise and Tite.

Who, what, where, how

The following 85 pages list all the clubs currently playing adult, male football on Lanzarote. They are set out in league order – Tercera, Interinsular and Lanzarote Regional – followed by other grounds, other clubs, disused grounds and former clubs.

Brief details about most clubs are included, together with their logo, shirt colours and a locator map to show roughly where they are in their locality. For the exact ground entrance details, use the What3words app – this is free to download.

Grounds shown are the usual home venue of that team but municipal grounds are used by several teams and some will play at more than one venue during the season, with various teams allocated to several. If you plan to watch a game, please check before travelling. Social media links are included where known – website and Facebook.

Admission prices are either for the 2021/22 season or the expected charge for 2022/23. All details are believed to be correct as at July 1, 2022.

The publisher bears no responsibility for any incorrect information. If you find an error, please contact the publisher for an amendment to be made in any reprints.

These initials are used throughout this book:

CD – Club Deportivo (Sport Club)

CF – Club de Fútbol (Football Club)

SCRD – Sociedad de Cultura, Recreo y Deportes (Society of Culture, Recreation and Sports)

UD – Unión Deportiva (Sports Union)

PDC – Puerto del Carmen

RFEF – Real Federación Española de Fútbol (Spanish Royal Football Federation)

c – circa

Arrecife
C
B
A
E
G
F
D
A Lanzarote
B Altavista
B Arrecife
C Tite
D Las Salinas
E Lomo
F Maciot
C Orientación
Marítima
E Municipal Stadium
C Estefut
G Torrelavega

Lanzarote

A Lanzarote
1 Union Sur Yaiza

2 San Bartolomé
3 Sporting Tías
4 Tahiche
5 Tinajo

B Altavista
B Arrecife
6 Haria
7 Inter Playa Honda
C Orientación Marítima
3 PDC Fútbol 2016
8 Puerto del Carmen
9 Teguise
C Tite

10 Club La Santa
11 Costa Teguise
12 Guatiza
D La Salinas
E Lomo
F Maciot
E Municipal Stadium

C Estefut

13 La Graciosa
14 Uga
G Torrelavega

Ciudad Deportiva de Lanzarote, main picture, and in its former guise as the roofless Estadio Avendaño Porrúa

Current league:
Tercera División RFEF,
Group 12 (Canary Islands)
(B team – Regional Division Lanzarote)

Formed: 1970

Ground address: Ciudad Deportiva de Lanzarote, Avenida Alcalde Ginés de la Hoz, 35500 Arrecife

main entrance reference: vine.boating.ruled

Ground's previous name:
Estadio Avendaño Porrúa (1968-1986)

Capacity: 6,000

Record crowd: 6,000 v Real Madrid, Copa Del Rey, November 2001.

Admission price: 8€

Car parking: On street

https://mercancialanzarote.com (English)

/LanzaroteFootballClub
/ptkudlanzarote
/groups/643407989922530

UD Lanzarote

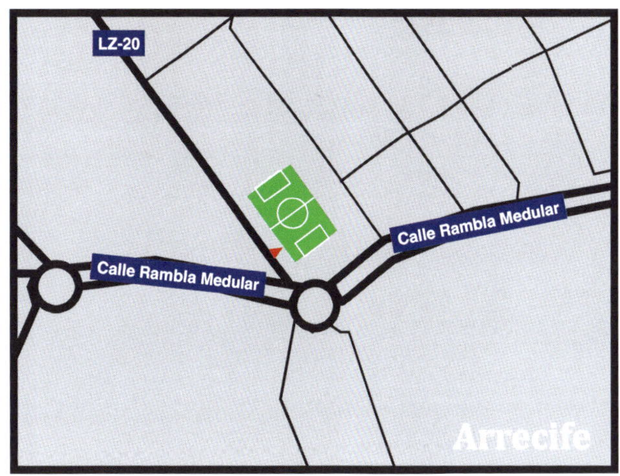

The marvellous stand at Ciudad Deportiva de Lanzarote, above, and left. The club's retail outlets, below – a shop in Costa Teguise and a market stall at Teguise market
Right: Fans fly the flag

UD Lanzarote

Clockwise from top left: British ex-pats form a large part of the fan base; entrance to the ground; clubhouse side; the far end

The Degollada volcano towers over Yaiza's municipal football ground

Current league:
Tercera División RFEF,
Group 12 (Canary Islands)

Formed: 1983

Ground address:
Fútbol Municipal de Yaiza,
Calle Vista de Yaiza, 11, 35570 Yaiza

main entrance reference:
ramming.shogun.guides

Capacity: c400

Record crowd:
Not known

Admission price: Not known

Car parking: Large car park

None found

/UnionSurYaiza

CD Union Sur Yaiza

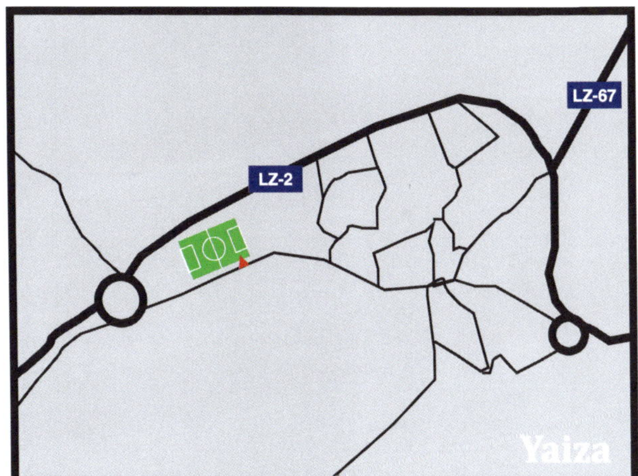

Tercera División

Ayuntamiento de Yaiza
CAMPO DE FUTBOL MUNICIPAL
DEPORTESYAIZA
MUNICIPIO ACTIVO

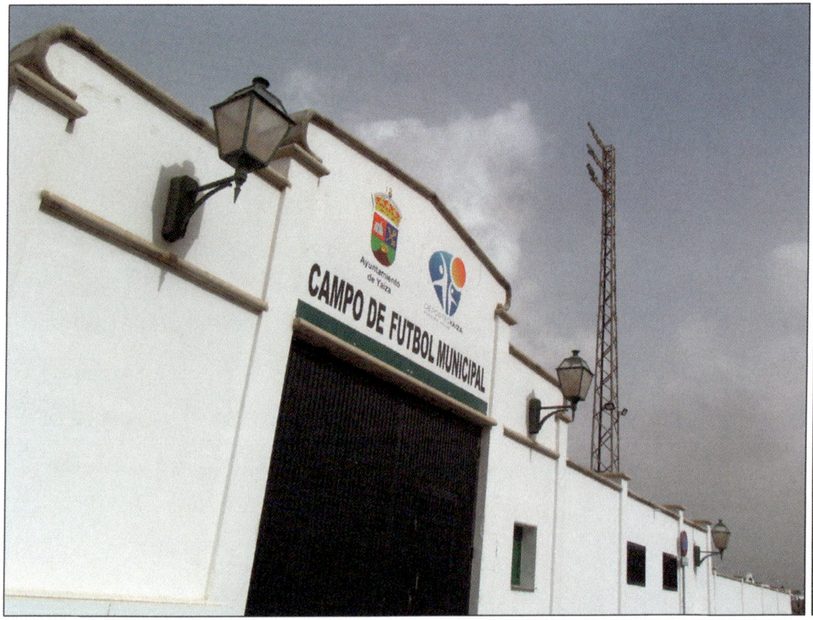

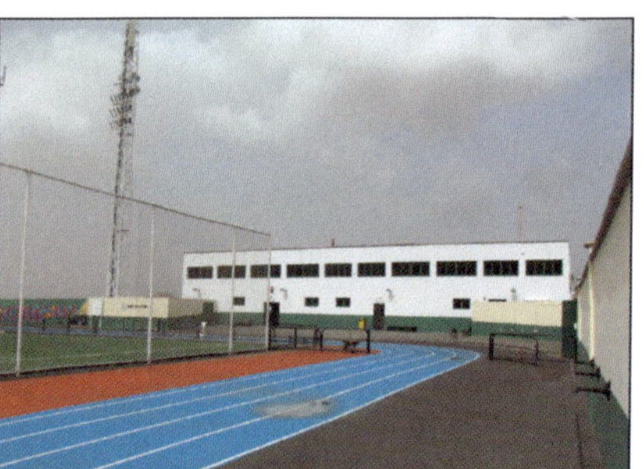

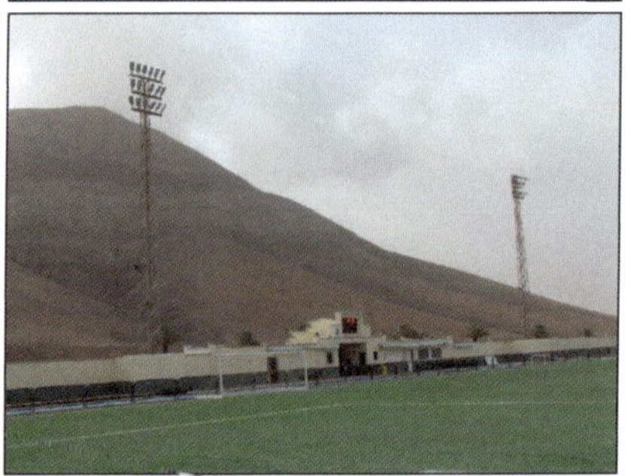

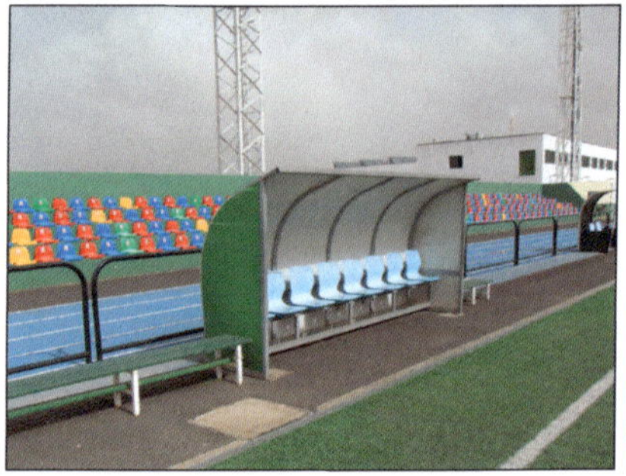

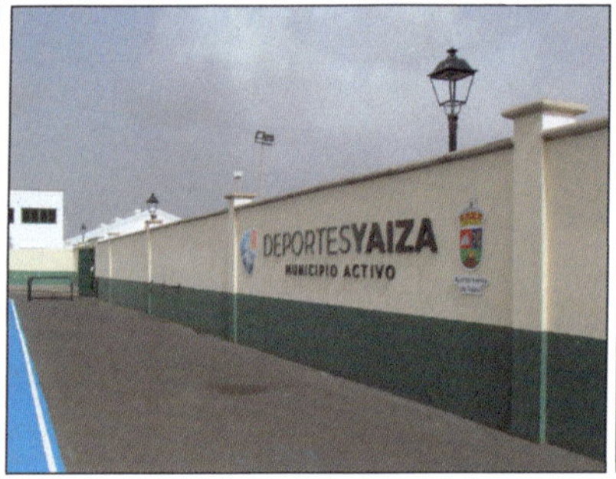

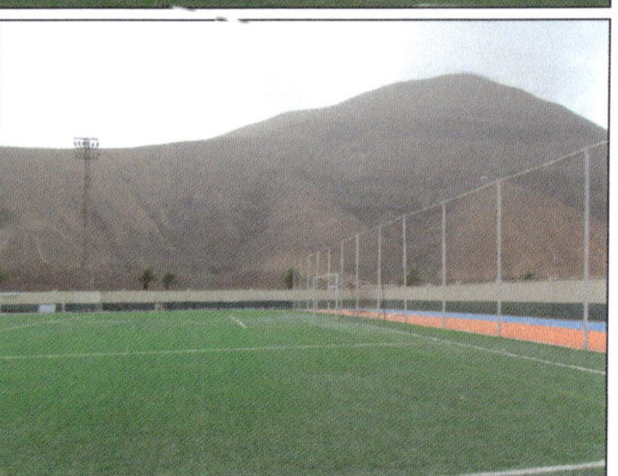

CD Union Sur Yaiza

Various views inside and around the municipal ground of CD Union Sur Yaiza

Mist out: San Bartolomé just missed out on a place in the 2022/23 Tercera División, losing in the play-offs after finishing second in the Interinsular División

Current league:
Preferente Interinsular
(B team – Regional Division Lanzarote)

Formed: 1972

Ground address: Campo Municipal de Fútbol Pedro Espinosa, Calle Pío XII 31, 35550 San Bartolomé

main entrance reference:
classy.initiates.ogre

Ground's previous name:
Las Palmeras

Capacity: c2,000. c750 seats

Record crowd: c1,400 v CD Union Puerto de Fuerteventura, 2011

Admission price: 4€

Car parking: On street

www.sanbartolomecf.com

/SanBartolomeCF

San Bartolomé CF

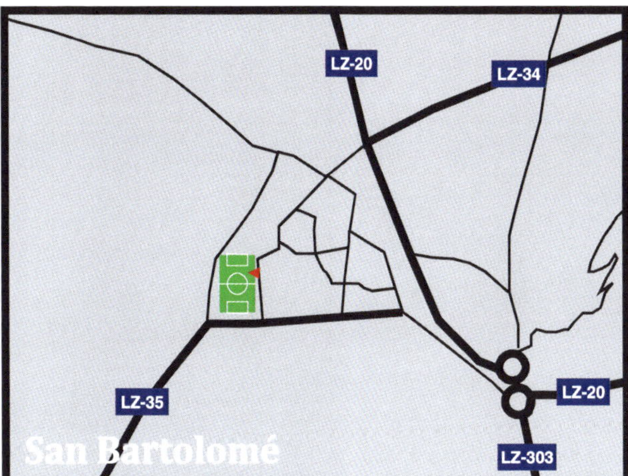

Inside and outside San Bartolomé's Campo Municipal de Fútbol Pedro Espinosa

San Bartolomé CF

Curve appeal: The Campo Municipal de Fútbol Francisco Bermudez Hernandez "Pancho"

CF Sporting Tías

Current league:
Preferente Interinsular

Formed: 1974

Ground address:
Campo Municipal de Fútbol Francisco Bermudez Hernandez "Pancho"
Calle Igualdad, 35572 Tías

main entrance reference:
trades.tester.splits

Capacity: 900. c660 seats

Record crowd: c800 v Unión Puerto (Fuerteventura), June 2010
(Ground record – c1,100 during time when UD Lanzarote were sharing)

Admission price: 5€

Car parking: Car park at ground

None found

/*clubdefutbolsportingtiasoficial*

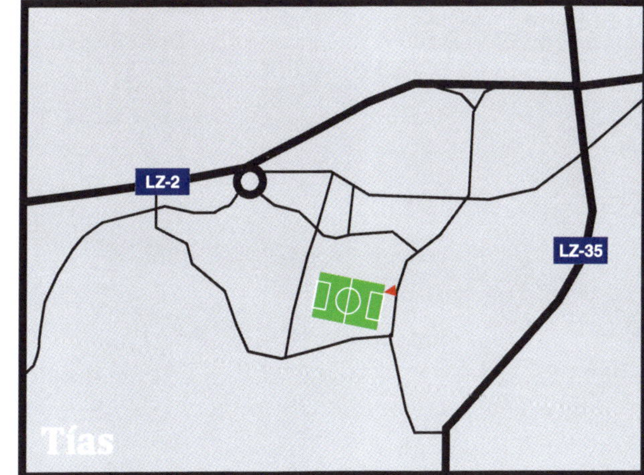

The Campo Municipal de Fútbol Francisco Bermudez Hernandez "Pancho" is attractive both inside and out

CF Sporting Tías

A volcanic view of the Campo de Fútbol at Tahiche

Current league:
Preferente Interinsular

Formed: 1973

Ground address:
Campo de Fútbol, Calle Rafael Alberti,
35507 Tahiche

main entrance reference:
cartoon.sparky.kindness

Capacity: c500 (c350 seats)

Record crowd: Not known

Admission price: c4-5€

Car parking: Steep car park at ground

None found

/cdtahiche

CD Tahiche

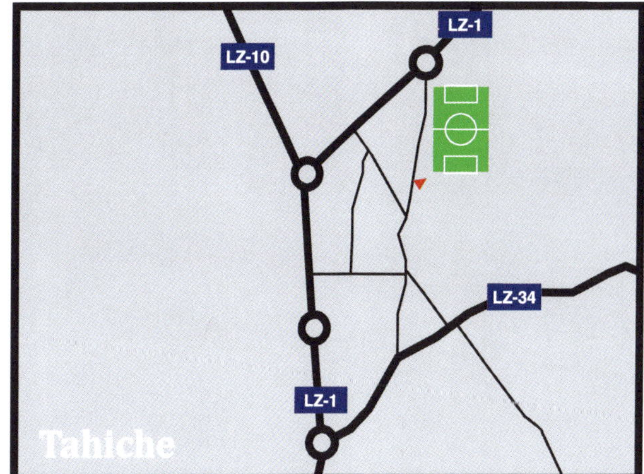

Behind closed doors: Access to the Campo de Fútbol at Tahiche proved elusive for the author. Luckily, the neighbouring volcano offered some great views over the walls

CD Tahiche

CD Tinajo's Los Volcanes Stadium attracts a large youth following, of both sexes

Current league:
Preferente Interinsular

Formed: 1975

Ground address: Los Volcanes, Campo de Fútbol Municipal de Tinajo, Avenida de los Volcanes, 35560 Tajaste

main entrance reference: risking.splitting.moreover

Capacity: 500 (can be extended with temporary stands)

Record crowd: 1,000 (with auxiliary stands), promotion play-off 2011, v Corralejo (Fuerteventura)

Admission price: Expected to be 4-5€

Car parking: Small car park at ground, street parking

www.cdtinajo.es

/CD-Tinajo-1596869660564544/

CD Tinajo

Tinajo's Campo de Fútbol Municipal comes alive under floodlights and will be hosting Preferente Interinsular football in 2022/23 after the club gained promotion via the Lanzarote Regional League play-offs

CD Tinajo

A new ground record was set at the Campo Municipal de Fútbol Agapito Reyes Viera for Altavista during the 2021/22 play-offs
Picture: Antonio Brito

Current league:
Regional Division Lanzarote

Formed: 1975

Ground address:
Campo Municipal de Fútbol Agapito Reyes Viera, Calle Mosta, 35500 Arrecife

main entrance reference:
record.dragon.sediment

Capacity: 390

Record crowd: 780 v CD Tinajo, Lanzarote League play-off, 2022

Admission price: 3€

Car parking: Limited street parking, large patch waste ground 100 metres away

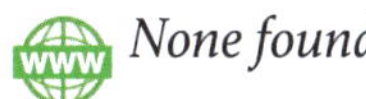
None found

/Altavistacf

Altavista CF

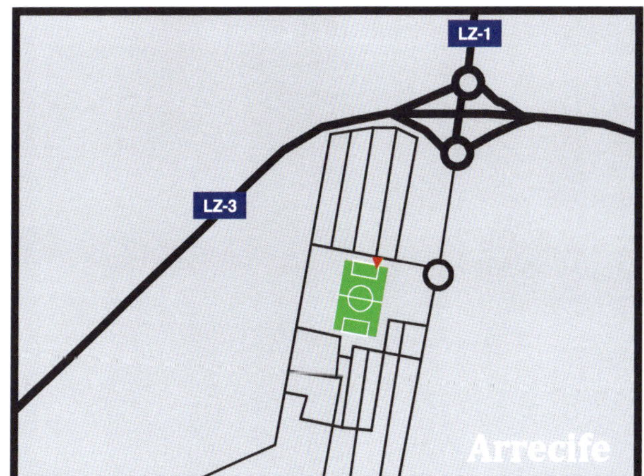

The Campo Municipal de Fútbol Agapito Reyes Viera before and after it was converted from a volcanic granular surface to artificial turf, top left and right

Action from Altavista's 1993 Interinsular League play-off against Pajara. That brought a record crowd of 632, which stood for 29 years

Pictures: Antonio Brito

Altavista CF

Altavista's Campo Municipal de Fútbol Agapito Reyes Viera home

CD Arrecife have shared Altavista's Campo Municipal de Fútbol Agapito Reyes Viera for a quarter-of-a-century

Current league:
Regional Division Lanzarote

Formed: 1964

Ground address:
Campo Municipal de Fútbol Agapito Reyes Viera, Calle Mosta, 35500 Arrecife (shared with Altavista for past 25 years)

main entrance reference:
record.dragon.sediment

Capacity: 390

Record crowd: Not known

Admission price: 3€

Car parking: Limited street parking, large patch waste ground 100 metres away

None found

/cdarrecife

CD Arrecife

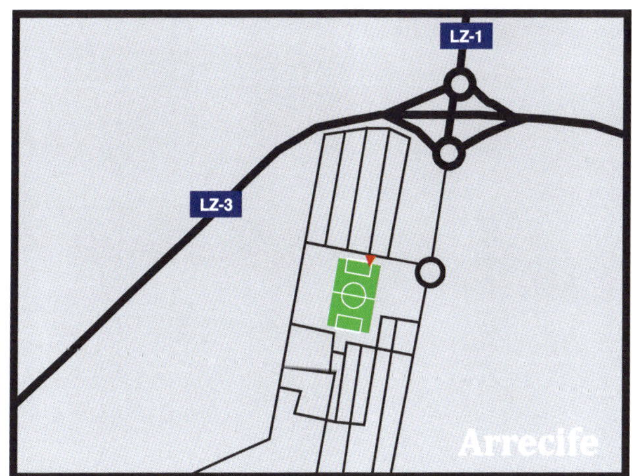

Haria CF's Campo de Fútbol Ladislao Rodriguez Bonilla is high in the mountains

Current league:
Regional Division Lanzarote

Formed: 1975

Ground address: Campo de Fútbol Ladislao Rodriguez Bonilla, Calle César Manrique, 19, 35520 Haría (Played at Guatiza 2001/2, while artificial pitch was laid)

main entrance reference: baubles.uncrowded.pods

Capacity: 500 (c200 seats)

Record crowd: Not known

Admission price: 3€

Car parking: Small car park and limited street parking

www.hariaclubdefutbol.com

/Hariaclubdefutbol

Haria CF

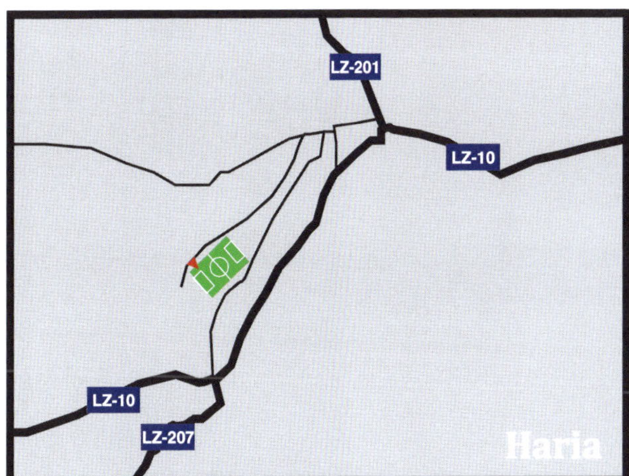

Regional Division Lanzarote

The Campo de Fútbol Ladislao Rodriguez Bonilla home of Haria adds a splash of colour to the grey landscape

Haria CF

Campo Municipal de Playa Honda was the last on the island to have artificial turf laid

Inter Playa Honda CF

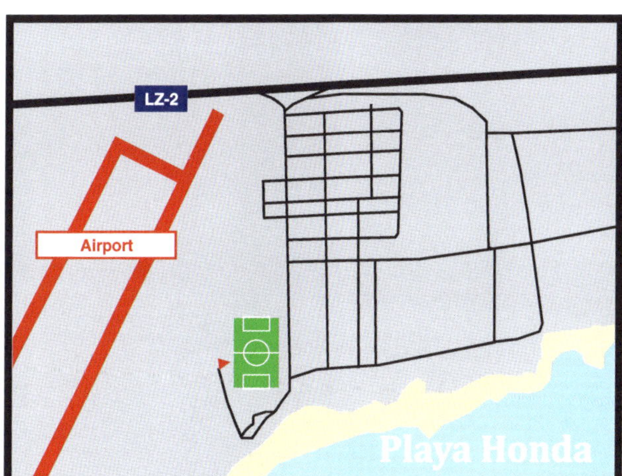

Current league:
Regional Division Lanzarote (2022/23 is their first season in the league since 2017)

Formed: 1994

Ground address:
Campo Municipal de Playa Honda,
35509 Playa Honda
(Last club on the island to switch to artificial grass – their last season on clay was 2006/7)

main entrance reference:
legislated.bystander.mercy

Capacity: c520

Record crowd: 982 v CD Tahiche, 2013

Admission price: Not applicable

Car parking: Large car park

www.interph.es/

/interplayahondaudlp

SANDOS

Inter Playa Honda

Campo Municipal de Playa Honda will be hosting regional league games for the first time in five years

Orient Marítima HQ

Ground address: Campo Municipal de Fútbol, José Díaz Contreras, Calle Guenia, 35500 Arrecife

Orientación Marítima headquarters and training pitch

/// what3words **main entrance reference:** disband.talents.wisely

Capacity: No spectator accommodation

Car parking: Street parking

Orientación Marítima do not use their HQ for league matches

Current league:
Regional Division Lanzarote

Formed: 1954

Ground address:
Orientación Marítima have no permanent home ground. The men's senior team usually play at Campo de Fútbol Municipal de Argana (CD Tite), youth teams at Ciudad Deportiva de Lanzarote (UD Lanzarote) or Campo de Fútbol Municipal Puerto Arrecife (CD Lomo). Campo Municipal de Fútbol Agapito Reyes Viera (Altavista) is also sometimes used. The women's team play at all four.

Record crowd: Not known

Admission price: 3€

www.futbolclubs.es/orientacionmaritima

/cdomaritima

Orientación Marítima

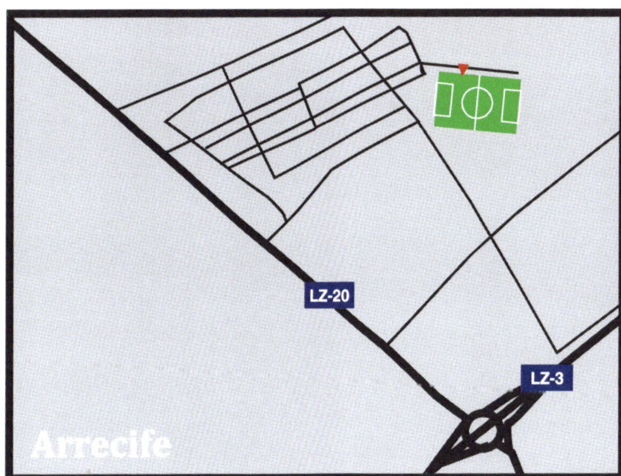

PDC Fútbol 2016 share the Campo de Fútbol Municipal de Tías with Sporting Tías

Current league:
Regional Division Lanzarote

Formed: 2016

Ground address:
Campo de Fútbol Municipal de Tías,
Calle Igualdad, 35572 Tías

main entrance reference:
trades.tester.splits

Capacity: 900. c660 seats

Record crowd: Not known

Admission price: 3€

Car parking: Car park at ground

None found

/cfutbolpdc2016

CF PDC Fútbol 2016

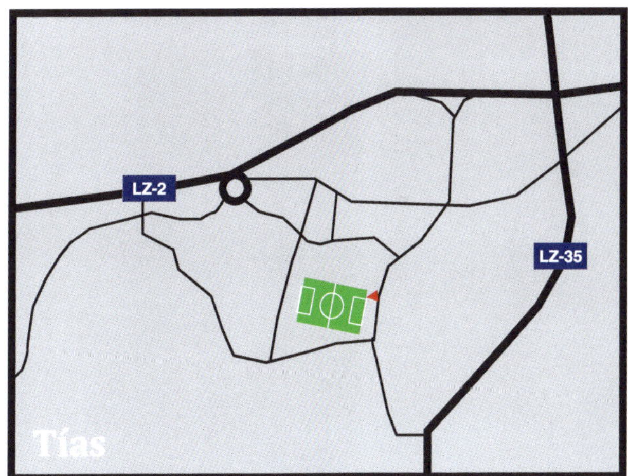

Estadio Municipal de Fútbol de Puerto del Carmen is a neat-looking ground

Current league:
Regional Division Lanzarote

Formed: 1982

Ground address: Estadio Municipal de Fútbol de Puerto del Carmen, Calle Rompimiento, 35510 Tías

main entrance reference: woodworker.restrict.pretty

Capacity: c750

Record crowd: Not known, set in 1984/5

Admission price: 3€

Car parking: Small car park at ground, street parking

None found

/FCPDClanza

FC Puerto del Carmen

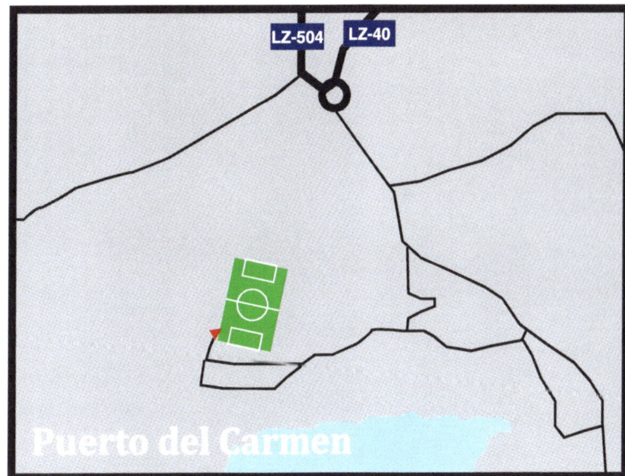

Estadio Municipal de Fútbol de Puerto del Carmen is tucked away on the western edge of the popular tourist destination

FC Puerto del Carmen

The Los Molinos Stadium lies in the shadow of Santa Bárbara Castle

Current league:
Regional Division Lanzarote

Formed: 1925

Ground address:
Los Molinos, Calle Gadifer de la Salle,
35530 Teguise

main entrance reference:
solar.bedding.collide

Capacity: 1,500 (c500 seats)

Record crowd: Not known

Admission price: 3€

Car parking: Large car park

None found

/Clubdeportivoteguise-343795119054915

CD Teguise

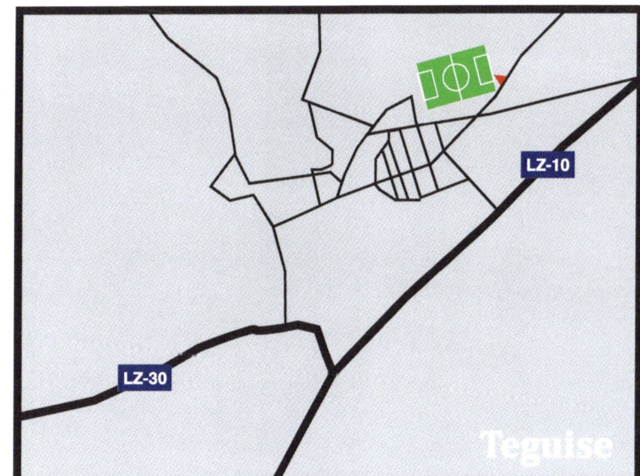

Regional Division Lanzarote

CD Teguise's Los Molinos Stadium – translates to 'The Mills'

CD Teguise

10,6 km
13,2 km
23,0 km
Teguise 1,0 km
San Bartolomé
Montaña Blanca

CAMPO DE FUTBOL LOS MOLINOS

CD Tite's Campo de Fútbol Municipal de Argan is one of several grounds in the city shared by other clubs

Current league:
Regional Division Lanzarote

Formed: 2010

Previous names:
1999-2010 Santa Coloma CF
(previously UD Puppetroy)
1997-1999 Unión Deportiva Titerroy

Ground address: Campo de Fútbol Municipal de Argana, Diseminado de las Laderas, 35500 Arrecife

what3words **main entrance reference:**
snapping.slice.behind

Capacity: 700

Record crowd: 700 v CD Tinajo, June 2022

Admission price: 3€

Car parking: Large car park

None found

/Club-Deportivo-Tite-120978801331889

CD Tite

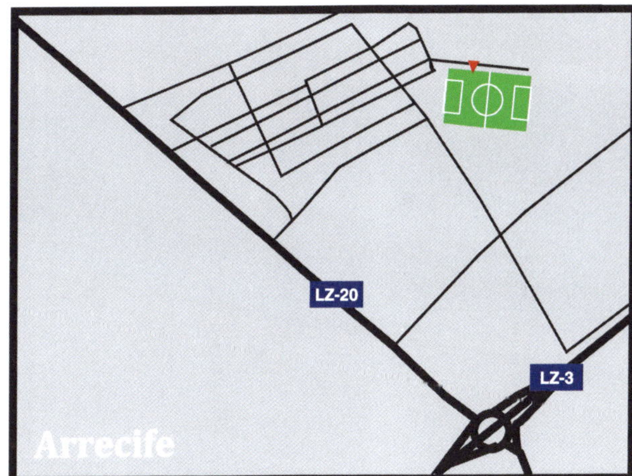

PUERTA 2

CD Tite

The Campo de Fútbol Municipal de Argana is in the northern suburbs of Arrecife and impossible to view from outside

Right, the club's 2021/22 record crowd

Picture: Antonio Brito

Some of Europe's top clubs have played on Club La Santa's unique grass pitch as part of their warm weather training

Club La Santa

Current league:
None – training camp, private resort

Formed: 1983

Ground address:
Avenida Krogager, La Santa, 35560

This is the only grass pitch on the island

main entrance reference:
sleeved.eclipses.moods

Capacity: Not known

Record crowd: None recorded

Admission price: Not applicable

www.clublasanta.co.uk

/ClubLaSanta

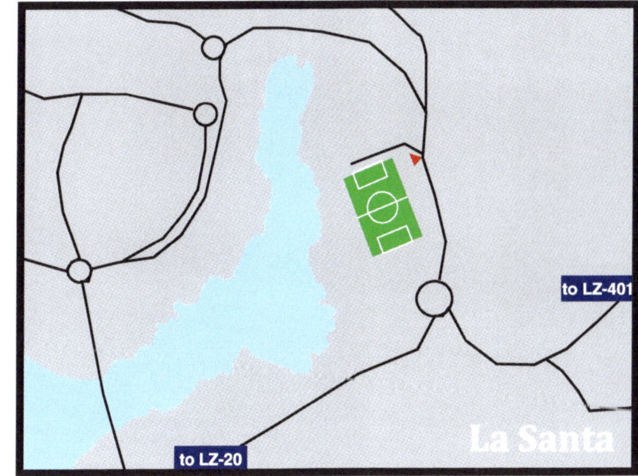

Work was progressing on a ground for UDP Costa Teguise in the summer of 2022
Pictures: Facebook @udpcostateguise

The site of UDP Costa Teguise's new ground
Pictures: Google Street View

Current league:
Youth only. Future plans for adult teams (Full name: UD Palmeiros Costa Teguise)

Formed: 2013

Ground address: Under construction. Corner of Calle Chafari and Calle Travesia del Hurón, 35508 Teguise

main entrance reference (approx): deems.lolly.bleak

Capacity: Not yet built

Record crowd: Not applicable

Admission price: Not applicable

Car parking: To be confirmed

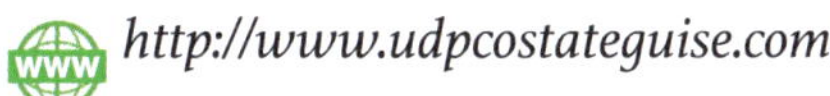

http://www.udpcostateguise.com/

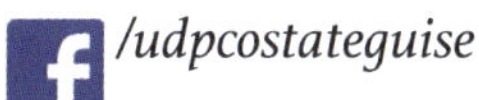

/udpcostateguise

UDP Costa Teguise

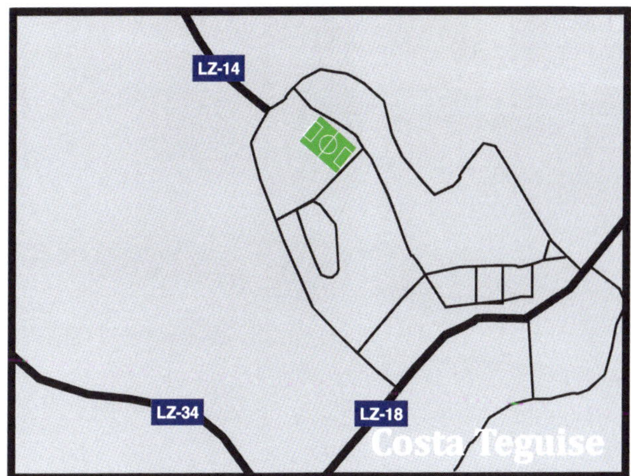

Guatiza's Calle Jesús María Betancort stadium is the last remaining on the island where games are played on volcanic granules

Current league:
Veterans only

Formed: Not known

Ground address:
Calle Jesús María Betancort, 35544 Guatiza
(Volcanic granule pitch)

main entrance reference:
dirt.loathes.outcome

Capacity: c300 seated

Record crowd: Not known

Admission price: Not applicable

Car parking: Street parking

None found

/guatiza.atletico

Guatiza

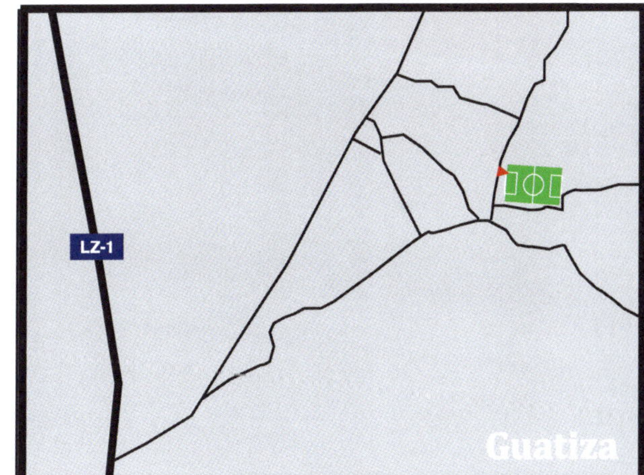

Guatiza

Guatiza's Calle Jesús María Betancort stadium has hosted Lanzarote League matches in the past

The Campo de Fútbol Las Salinas is hidden away in Arrecife's streets, just round the corner from the headquarters of Orientación Marítima

Ground address:
Campo de Fútbol Las Salinas, Caldera de Taburiente, 35507 Las Salinas, Arrecife

main entrance reference:
rail.starred.shin

Capacity: Pitchside standing only

Car parking: Street parking

Campo de Fútbol Las Salinas is the least used of Lanzarote's grounds for adult football

Las Salinas

Other grounds

CD Lomo are one of many city teams who call the Campo de Fútbol Municipal Puerto Arrecife home

Current league:
Youth only
Played in Regional League until 2012

Formed: 1954

Ground address:
Campo de Fútbol Municipal Puerto Arrecife, Calle Chafaris, 3550 Arrecife

main entrance reference:
snatched.staked.vitamins

Capacity: c600 (c400 seats)

Record crowd: Not known

Admission price: Not applicable

Car parking: Large car park

None found

/Club-Deportivo-LOMO-1599776173998 57

CD Lomo

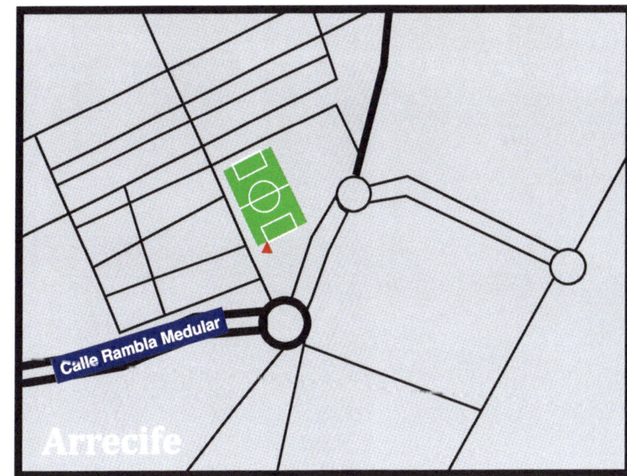

Other grounds

The Port of Arrecife Municipal ground is centrally located, just along from UD Lanzarote's Ciudad Deportiva de Lanzarote

CD Lomo

A number of Arrecife clubs have played 'home' matches at the Campo de Fútbol de San Francisco Javier

Current league:
Youth, veteran and training only

Formed: 2006

Ground address:
Campo de Fútbol de San Francisco Javier, Calle de Alfonso XIII, 53, 35509 Arrecife

The ground was inaugurated in May 2007 with a match between UD Lanzarote and Orientación Marítima. Regional League matches have been played when the Argana municipal field was being fitted with artificial turf and CD Tite played some matches here, as did Haria youth teams when their ground was being built

main entrance reference:
napkins.bunkers.voltage

Capacity: c500 (c250 seats)

Record crowd: Not known

Admission price: Not applicable

Car parking: Street parking

None found

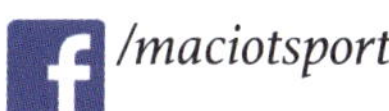
/maciotsport

CD Maciot Sport

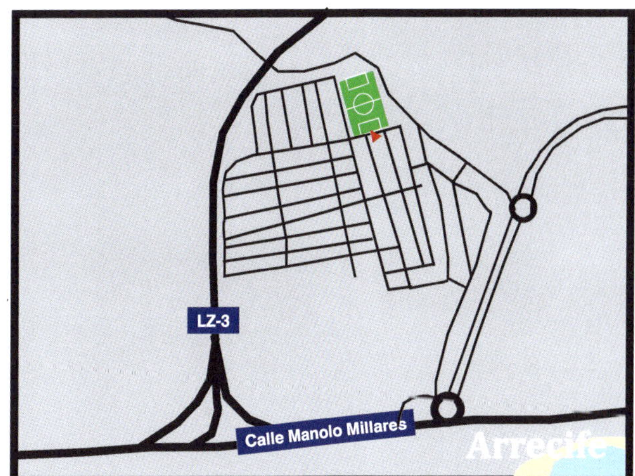

The Campo de Fútbol de San Francisco Javier is built into the side of a hill and offers great street-level views

CD Maciot Sport

Close investigation of Google Street View images revealed another ground on the island – albeit just a pair of goalposts.

Standing forlornly alongside the Playa de la Garita off the LZ-1 road (directly opposite the LZ-207), they are barely a throw-in away from the surf.

Unfortunately, a visit to the scene revealed the posts are no longer standing and the only information found suggested it had been there about 30 years ago. The ground consisted of only a pitch and goalposts but some tournaments were played there.

Just to complete the set, here are Google Map and Street View images of Lanzarote's 'other' ground:

The mystery ground

Other clubs

Current league:
Youth only

Formed: 2010

Ground address: Campo de Fútbol Municipal de Argana, Diseminado de las Laderas, 35500 Arrecife

main entrance reference:
snapping.slice.behind

Capacity: c400

Record crowd: Not known

Admission price: Not applicable

Car parking: Large car park

None found

/estefut

CD Estefut

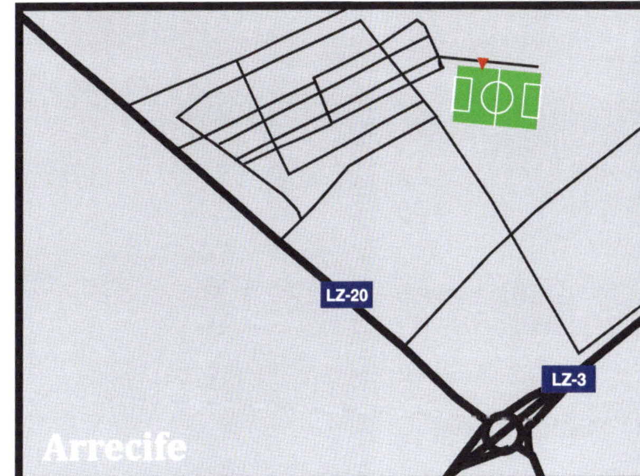

Floodlights and pylons, as well as a football pitch-sized area of flat land, mark the spot where CD Atlético Uga played

Disused grounds

Current league:
None – folded

Formed: Not known
Played in Regional League until 2008

Ground address (abandoned):
Calle Montaña Mesa, 35570 Uga

main entrance reference:
burning.gills.backdrop

Capacity: Not known

Record crowd: Not known

Admission price: Not applicable

Car parking: Street parking

None found

None found

CD Atlético Uga

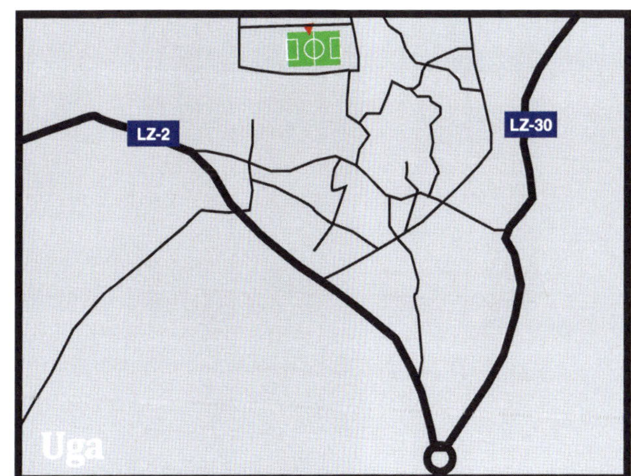

Goalposts and floodlights remain in place at Caleta del Sebo but the pitch is now little more than a public dumping ground Picture: Google Street View

Current league:
None – former youth teams

Formed: 1965
Folded: 1980s

Ground address: Calle Escota, 35540 Caleta del Sebo, La Graciosa

main entrance reference: seafront.plankton.tenant

Capacity: Not known

Record crowd: Not known

Admission price: Not applicable

Car parking: Only licenced vehicles are allowed on the island for special purposes

 None found

 None found

La Graciosa is one of the last places in Europe with no asphalted roads. It is the least explored of the Canary Islands. Access to the island, which is 1.25 miles north of Lanzarote across the Strait of El Río, is by a 25-minute ferry crossing from Órzola to Caleta del Sebo harbour.

La Graciosa

Several attempts have been made to form a club on the island, starting in 1965 when Swedish visitor Lemar Vicent created three youth teams. In the mid-1970s Royal Graciosa were started and played in youth tournaments on Lanzarote. In 2013 CD Teguise launched a joint project and CD Teguise-La Graciosa played as a youth team. A ground was built in the 1980s but it is now abandoned and used as a rubbish tip.
A futsal team was formed and played in the Lanzarote League in 2021/22.

All that remains of the Calle Dr Gómez Ulla home of SCRD Torrelavega

Current league:
None – folded

Formed: 1944
Folded: 2010

Ground address (abandoned):
Calle Dr Gómez Ulla, 35500 Arrecife

main entrance reference (approx):
magnets.gear.neon

Capacity: Not known

Record crowd: Not known

Admission price: Not applicable

None found

/scrd.torrelavega

SCRD Torrelavega

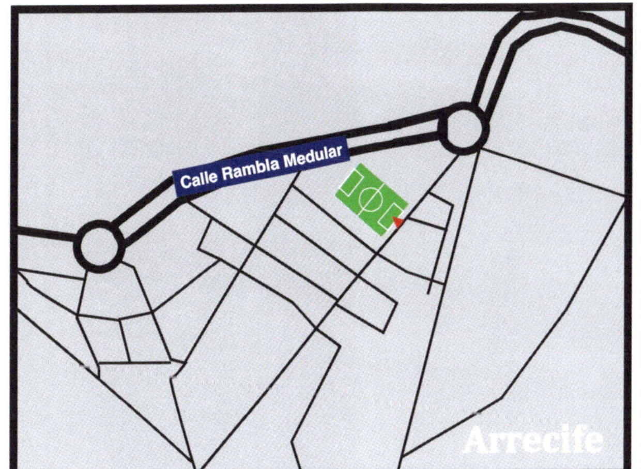

The following clubs are no longer playing adult football or have folded:

Afrocán (1991-92)

The club shared with Altavista at the Campo Municipal de Fútbol Agapito Reyes Viera.

The team was created by a group of friends but only competed for one season in the Lanzarote Regional League

Atlético Tiense (2004 to 2013)

Matches were played at the Municipal Field of Tías. They were formed to accommodate the players of the municipality who could not or did not want to play for CF Sporting Tías or FC Puerto del Carmen.

Twitter: @AtleticoTiense

UD La Asomada (1991-97)

Matches were played at the Municipal Field of Tías

CF La Plaza (to 1993)

Matches were played at the Ciudad Deportiva Lanzarote and the Campo Municipal de Argana. They eventually joined forces with CD Santa Coloma, which later evolved into CD Tite.

 http://laplazacf.es.tl

 /laplazacf

CD Santa Maria de la Vega (to 2018 as an adult side –now as a new unrelated junior club playing out of San Bartolomé)

The Lanzarote Regional League side played in the Ciudad Deportiva Lanzarote (formerly Avendaño Porrua) and in the Municipal de Argana

 /CD-Sta-Maria-de-La-Vega-1741078989543343/

UD Valterra (to 2006)

They trained in a field that was located in the Valterra neighbourhood at what is today a petrol station and the ambulatory. They played their regional and youth league fixtures at the Ciudad Deportiva Lanzarote.

Shop front

Many of Lanzarote's senior teams have a clubhouse with a bar and, sometimes a shop. UD Lanzarote have their own club shop in Costa Teguise, as well as a market stall at Teguise market (see Page 24).

The bar at Haria

The retail offering at CF Sporting Tías

Expect an increase in sales at CD Tinajo, above, following their promotion

The canteen at the Campo Municipal de Fútbol Agapito Reyes Viera, right, serves fans of both Altavista CF and CD Arrecife

The day the giants landed on Lanzarote

November 27, 2001, is a date that is carved into Lanzarote folklore. That was the day the giants of Real Madrid came to the island to take on UD Lanzarote in the Copa del Ray. Newly promoted to Segunda División B as Tercera champions, the Rojillos hit the jackpot on their return to the Spanish Cup when they drew the illustrious Galacticos at home in Arrecife.

While Lanzarote would go on to finish eighth in their league, Real Madrid were crowned Europe's No.1 for the ninth time, after beating Bayer Leverkusen in the Champions League final. The visitors might have had 28 La Liga titles and 17 Copa del Rays to their name but on that red-hot Canarian evening, the teams were on the same stage, starting equal.

Lanzarote had already claimed a huge scalp by seeing off island rivals Tenerife in sensational style; local legend Maciot bagging a hat-trick in his team's 5-1 victory. The reward for that remarkable feat was a dream come true for any football fan – a date with one of the most famous clubs in world football.

Real Madrid were taking the game seriously and stars such as Zinédine Zidane, Luís Figo, Claude Makélélé and Steve McManaman arrived to star in UD Lanzarote's grandest game ever.

In front of a full house, Vicente Del Bosque's Galacticos took the lead on the half-hour mark when Santiago Solari headed on for Albert Celados to tap in.

Would it be a case of trying to keep count of many more goals hit the back of the home net?

No, that was far from reality as the minnows hit back shortly before half-time when local boy and part-time waiter Oscar Vladimir equalised with a right-foot shot from Francis Santana's header to

World Cup and Champions League winner and three-times world footballer of the year Zinédine Zidane prepares to enter the fray Picture: Courtesy of UD Lanzarote/Insular Audiovisuales Video

secure his place in Lanzarote football history.

The visitors had to dig deep after the break and goals from Guti and Francisco Pavón eventually saw them run out 3-1 winners.

Madrid's starting line-up on that night consisted of 10 full international players – six Spanish, an Argentinian, a Cameroonian, one English and one French. Added to that, the two substitutes they used eventually retired with 235 full caps between them for Portugal (Figo) and France (Zidane) respectively.

That Real team comprised: César Sánchez, Njitap Geremi, Raúl Bravo, Aitor Karanka, Pavón, Makélélé, Albert Celades, Santiago Solari, McManaman, Pedro Munitis and captain Guti. Zidane replaced Solari, while Figo came on for McManaman.

Up against them, the home ranks consisted of Marino, Carlitos, Pero Cruz, Armanda Tejera, Ismael Arroyo, Zipi, Saulo Alonso, Vladimir Ramos, Fali, Francis Santana and Jonathan Torres. Their substitutes were Ito, Maciot and Santi Torres.

UD Lanzarote had another chance of causing a Copa del Ray upset in 2003/4 when they were again drawn at home to La Liga giants, this time in the shape of Sevilla.

However, on this occasion they were to lose home advantage as Spain's oldest football club refused to

The teams pose for pre-match pictures

Pictures: Courtesy of UD Lanzarote/Insular Audiovisuales Video

play on Lanzarote's artificial surface and the tie was switched to Gran Canaria.

More than 5,000 Lanzarote supporters watched the islanders perform valiantly and only a goal from Julio Baptista separated the sides. The dream got better in 2004 when Lanzarote beat Mallorca 2-1 thanks to goals from Alyson and Di Renzo.

Athletic Club Bilbao were the next Primera Liga side to taste Lanzarote's thirst for the Copa del Ray as Alejandro scored twice to sink them 2-1 the following year. However, in the return leg in Bilbao, the Basque team made no mistake and broke the Rojillos' hearts of their dream of reaching the quarter-finals with a 6-0 thumping.

● View match highlights of Lanzarote's tie with Real Madrid on YouTube – *tinyurl.com/*LanzReal

Match report details courtesy of Ian Lane and the *https://mercancialanzarote.com* website

Lanzarote celebrate the goal from Oscar Vladimir

Pictures: Courtesy of UD Lanzarote/Insular Audiovisuales Video

Fans found vantage points anywhere they could

Appendix

Lanzarote teams' pitches are made of artificial turf but there's still a need for a spade and wheelbarrow, as this image at Yaiza shows

The last 32 seasons (2021/2-2006/7)

	21/2	20/1	19/0	18/9	17/8	16/7	15/6	14/5	13/4	12/3	11/2	10/1	09/0	08/9	07/8	06/7
Altavista	D1	D8	D11	D8	D4	D10	D8	D10	D11	D9	D8	C18	C11	C10	C5	C6
Arrecife	D7	D4	D10	D3	D6	D5	D7	D7	D9	D5	D6	D9	D6	D8	D9	D10
Atlético Tiense	x	x	x	x	x	x	x	x	x	C18	D1	D4	C16	C14	C6	D1
Atlético Uga	x	x	x	x	x	x	x	x	x	x	x	x	x	x	D6	D9
Haria	D11	D6	D3	C16	B21	C2	C10	D4	D2	D1	D10	D5	C17	D4	D2	D7
Lanzarote	B11	B6	B14	B5	B4	B12	B2	B2	B11	B14	B5	B1	A20	A14	A13	A12
Lanzarote B	D5	x	D7	D9	x	x	x	x	x	x	D5	x	x	D6	D5	D12
Lomo	x	x	x	x	x	x	x	x	x	x	D9	D6	D8	D5	D11	D14
Orientación Marítima	D3	D3	D8	x	x	D7	D9	x	x	x	x	B18	B13	B11	B8	A19
Orientación Mar B.	x	x	x	x	x	x	x	x	x	x	x	x	x	x	x	D13
Playa Honda	x	x	x	x	x	D3	x	D8	D6	D4	D11	D8	D7	D10	x	D11
Puerto Del Carmen	D10	D9	D2	D6	D2	D1	D4	D3	D4	D10	x	x	D10	D11	D10	D15
San Bartolomé	C2	C8	D1	D2	D1	C15	D1	D2	D3	C15	C6	D1	D4	D3	D8	D4
San Bartolomé B	D8	x	x	x	x	D9	x	x	x	x	x	x	x	x	x	x
Santa Maria dl Vega	x	x	x	x	D9	x	x	x	x	x	x	x	x	x	D13	D16
Sporting Tías	C6	D1	D4	D7	D7	D8	D3	D5	D8	D7	D7	C17	D2	D7	D7	D8
Sporting Tías B.	x	x	x	x	x	x	x	x	x	x	x	D7	x	x	x	x

	21/2	20/1	19/0	18/9	17/8	16/7	15/6	14/5	13/4	12/3	11/2	10/1	09/0	08/9	07/8	06/7
Tahiche	C4	C4	C19	D1	C17	D4	C15	C8	D1	D2	D2	D3	D5	D2	D1	D2
Teguise	D9	D10	D6	D5	D5	C18	D2	D6	D7	D6	C17	C14	C10	B20	B7	B13
Tinajo	D4	D5	D5	D4	D3	D2	D6	D1	D5	D8	D2	D2	D1	C17	D3	D3
Tinajo B	x	x	x	x	x	x	x	x	x	x	x	x	x	D9	x	x
Tite	D2	D2	D9	D10	D8	D6	D5	D9	D10	D3	D4	D10	x	x	x	x
(Santa Coloma)	x	x	x	x	x	x	x	x	x	x	x	x	D9	D13	D12	D5
Torrelavega	x	x	x	x	x	x	x	x	x	x	x	x	D3	D1	D4	D6
Yaiza	B6	C1	C9	B18	B10	B7	B11	B5	B9	C2	C4	C8	C3	C13	C11	B21

KEY:
A: Segunda B
B: Tercera
C: Interinsular
D: Lanzarote Regional
The number denotes finishing position

The last 32 seasons (2005/6-1990/1)

	05/6	04/5	03/4	02/3	01/2	00/1	99/0	98/9	97/8	96/7	95/6	94/5	93/4	92/3	91/2	90/1
Afrocán	x	x	x	x	x	x	x	x	x	x	x	x	x	x	D17	x
Altavista	C7	C11	C9	C13	C11	D1	D4	D5	D1	D1	D6	D4	C17	D3	D4	D4
Arrecife	D17	D13	D8	D7	D8	D9	D12	D13	D14	D10	D8	D11	D11	D16	D9	D7
Atlético Tiense	D5	D4	x	x	x	x	x	x	x	x	x	x	x	x	x	x
Haria	D3	D1	D1	D1	D6	D2	D3	D4	D4	D8	D7	D9	D8	D11	D2	D14
La Asomada	x	x	x	x	x	x	x	x	x	D14	D12	D16	D15	D10	D14	x
Lanzarote	A11	A13	A1	A3	A8	B1	A17	B3	B4	B8	B13	C1	B18	B16	C3	C3
Lanzarote B	D8	x	x	C18	D2	D8	D1	x	x	x	x	x	x	x	x	x
Lanzarote Atlético	x	x	x	x	x	x	x	x	x	x	x	x	D14	x	x	x
Lomo	D7	D5	D10	D10	D9	D13	D14	D12	D12	D13	D13	D13	D16	D8	D15	D12
Orientación Marítima	B3	B4	B11	B9	B10	B10	B10	C1	C7	C4	D2	D1	D5	D1	D1	C18
Orientación Mar B.	D14	D10	D5	D9	x	x	x	x	x	x	x	x	x	x	x	x
Playa Honda	D9	x	x	x	x	x	x	x	x	x	D15	D17	x	x	x	x
Puerto Del Carmen	D15	D11	D11	D8	D11	D7	D7	D9	D8	D11	D11	D12	D9	D9	D3	D13
San Bartolomé	D10	D7	D9	D11	D5	D4	D11	D1	D7	D7	D3	D8	D2	D2	D5	D11
Santa Maria dl Vega	D16	D14	D12	D12	D12	D10	D13	D10	D11	D12	C16	D3	D6	D6	D8	D15
Sporting Tías	D1	D2	D6	D4	D10	D12	D8	D11	D9	D2	D1	D5	D4	D15	D10	D6

	05/6	04/5	03/4	02/3	01/2	00/1	99/0	98/9	97/8	96/7	95/6	94/5	93/4	92/3	91/2	90/1
Tahiche	D6	D3	D4	D5	D1	D6	D10	D3	D10	D5	D9	D6	D3	D4	D11	D3
Teguise	B9	B17	B10	B15	C2	C14	C13	C11	C9	D4	D4	C17	C7	C12	C2	D1
Teguise Atlético	x	D12	D12	x	x	x	x	x	x	x	x	D14	D13	D13	x	x
Tinajo	D4	D6	D7	D6	D7	D11	D6	D7	D5	D3	D10	D7	D7	D7	D13	D9
Tite	x	x	x	x	x	x	x	x	x	x	x	x	x	x	x	x
(La Plaza)	x	x	x	x	x	x	x	x	x	x	x	x	x	D12	D12	D8
(Santa Coloma)	D2	D9	D3	D3	D4	D5	D9	x	x	x	x	x	x	x	x	x
(Titerroy)	x	x	x	x	x	x	x	D14	D13	D16	D16	D15	D12	D17	D16	D10
Torrelavega	D11	C16	D2	D2	D3	D3	D2	D8	D6	D9	D5	D2	D1	D5	D6	D5
Valterra	D13	D8	x	x	D14	D14	D5	D6	D1	C16	C13	C5	C4	C6	C9	C7
Yaiza	C2	C3	C3	C3	C8	C6	C5	D2	D3	D6	D14	D10	D10	D14	D7	D2
Yaiza B	x	x	x	D13	D13	x	x	x	x	x	x	x	x	x	x	x

KEY:

A: Segunda B

B: Tercera

C: Interinsular

D: Lanzarote Regional

The number denotes finishing position

Getting there

Club transport at CD Arrecife, right, and Haria CF, below

Distances between league grounds

Kilometres above the X diagonal; approximate minutes by car below it.

		Arrecife/Altavista	Haria	Inter Playa Honda	Lanzarote	Municipal Stadium	Puerto del Carmen	San Bartolomé	Tahiche	Teguise	Tías/PDC 2016	Tinajo	Tite/Marítima	Yaiza
		1	2	3	4	5	6	7	8	9	10	11	12	13
1	Arrecife/Altavista	X	33	8	3	2	19	10	11	21	12	21	3	27
2	Haria	35	X	35	31	30	45	26	23	15	40	34	31	43
3	Inter Playa Honda	10	37	X	6	6	13	9	16	18	9	24	7	21
4	Lanzarote	5	31	11	X	1	16	9	8	16	11	20	3	24
5	Municipal Stadium	5	34	10	2	X	16	8	7	12	11	20	3	24
6	Puerto del Carmen	13	36	17	17	17	X	14	22	28	6	18	17	14
7	San Bartolomé	13	33	15	11	11	16	X	12	13	8	14	7	20
8	Tahiche	14	22	16	10	12	22	13	X	10	18	23	9	30
9	Teguise	24	22	20	18	17	27	17	11	X	18	22	17	31
10	Tías/PDC 2016	14	38	11	12	13	8	9	17	21	X	16	12	14
11	Tinajo	23	41	27	21	24	22	16	22	24	19	X	18	16
12	Tite/Marítima	6	33	13	5	7	17	10	12	20	12	20	X	25
13	Yaiza	27	50	24	23	25	18	20	28	34	16	20	25	X

This is Lanzarote

Lanzarote offers all-year sunshine and is a popular winter sun destination for UK travellers. With a daytime average temperature of 22-24 degrees Celsius in January (and often up to 28), it offers the chance to recharge post-Christmas batteries.

Serious tourism on the island did not take off until the early 1980s, after the introduction of package holidays in the late '70s. Despite the tourism boom of the 1960s on other Canary islands, holiday development on Lanzarote had been slow. By that time, the local government (El Cabildo) started to put an emphasis on improving the infrastructure, including an extension of the airport runway to allow for international flights. Today, more than one and a half million tourists visit the island each year, the majority coming from Great Britain, Germany and continental Spain.

... and chill!

Lanzarote is different to other sun and sea destinations and is proud to claim it is a place where nature and art prevail – pushing The Lanzarote Effect as a place where the people are as warm as they are active and proud; where the food tastes of the sea and the earth; where the essence of the island leaves a mark on your soul long after you depart. This unique island has everything – stunning volcanic landscapes, amazing nature attractions, picturesque sandy beaches, attractive luxury hotels, interesting places to see and plenty of great things to do. On top of all this, there is an abundance of tasty gastronomy. Over the years many natural sights have been transformed into spectacular tourist attractions, including the Jameos del Agua, the Cueva de los Verdes, Mirador del Río and the Timanfaya National Park.

Oh, and there's plenty of live football to watch too!

Thanks and recommended websites

My thanks go to everyone who has contributed in the production of this book. All contributions have been gratefully received in putting this publication together:

Antonio Brito (Altavista and island football in general), Ian Lane (UD Lanzarote), Sergio Diaz De Rojas (UDP Costa Teguise), Elena Fuentes (CD Teguise), Marcial Cedrés (CD Arrecife), Montse Parrizas (Club La Santa), Arminda Delgado (Cabolt Lanzarote), Irene Gómez (César Manrique Foundation), Vicente Masia Pous (Spanish Football Encyclopedia) Augustine Hernandez, Sarabel and Chino (the Web de Lanzarote), Jordan Penny (graphics), Jim Stewart (Football Weekends magazine).

Google Street View, Google Maps, Facebook *@udpcostateguise*, Insular Audiovisuales Video, *mercancialanzarote.com* and to all the club officials, groundstaff and council workers who made me welcome on my unannounced arrival at their stadiums. Apologies to anyone I might have missed but rest assured your contribution was equally appreciated.

I recommend any of the following websites to help you discover more about football on Lanzarote – many are in Spanish but Google Translate is your friend! – *tinyurl.com/TranslateESUK*

- Encyclopedia of Spanish football – *lafutbolteca.com*
- Las Palmas Football (inc Lanzarote) – *futbolaspalmas.com/1preferenteint*
- Spanish FA – *rfef.es*
- Canarian Football Asociation – *http://federacioncanariafutbol.es/*
- Follow Your League – *siguetuliga.com/region/canarias*
- Spanish Regional Football – *futbol-regional.es*
- Lanzarote Sport – *lanzarotedeportiva.com*
- Cricket on Lanzarote – *cricketspain.es/es/a-brief-history-of-lanzarote-cricket-pete-starmer*
- Lanzarote Web – *webdelanzarote.com*
- Lanzarote Information (in English) – *lanzaroteinformation.co.uk*
- Bus routes and times – *lanzaroteguide.com/lanzarote-bus-routes-and-timetables*

All links were working July 2022 but the publisher takes no responsibility for any broken links or out-of-date content on these sites and pages.

Also by this author

Towering Tales & a Ripping Yarn – Yorkshire football's grassroots legends

Football writer Steven Penny takes you on a journey across the football fields of Yorkshire during the 2020/21 season, discovering some incredible links to the game's greats.

Liverpool, Manchester United and Arsenal are among 90 professional clubs from the UK who have links to the lower-level Yorkshire clubs featured in this book. Add a sprinkle of overseas clubs and international teams, including England's 1966 World Cup winners, and the grassroots scene in the Broad Acres has given much to the global game.

Discover the story of the world's first black professional footballer, the pop star who arranged his gigs to carry on playing Sunday football and the White Rose apprenticeship served by managerial legends Bill Shankly, Joe Harvey and Herbert Chapman. Read about the schoolboy footballers who conquered the world and the fictional team that went down a storm in a TV classic.

Penny digs up dozens of tremendous tales of life on the White Rose county's lesser-known football fields. **£11.99/£9.99**

Soap Stars & Burst Bubbles – A season of Yorkshire football

Football writer Steven Penny takes you on a journey across the football fields of Yorkshire during the 2002/03 season. From the multi-national squad of Premiership club Middlesbrough to the six-year-old boys of Wheldrake Junior FC playing their first game.

The book concentrates on the non-League clubs of the county, from Barnoldswick – playing in Lancashire competitions – to Easington – tucked away on Spurn Point. And from Northern League sides Marske United and Northallerton Town to the world's oldest club, Sheffield FC, now based in Derbyshire.

Penny reports on more than 40 matches, including Harrogate Railway's remarkable FA Cup run and Doncaster Rovers' return to the Football League. As well as reports and match details from every game, included are club histories, interviews with fans and club officials as well as stories from Penny's trips around the county and his long non-League football pedigree. **£10.99/£9.99**

Both books are available from Amazon as paperback or ebooks

Also by this author

Tarts, Trams and Tuk Tuks – A Lisbon football weekend

Travel writer Steven Penny discovers the delights of football and more in and around the Portuguese capital. After an opening night's death-defying dash only to be refused entry by a belligerent security guard it had to get better… didn't it?

Available direct from the author via eBay – £6 plus £1.65 UK postage
tinyurl.com/TartsTuk

Coming soon…

Pilgrims' Patch

– The football grounds of Lincolnshire

Enjoy yourself on a journey across almost 50 venues throughout the county of Lincolnshire – from Barton Town in the north to Long Sutton Athletic in the south and across from Crowle to Skegness Town.

Includes the Football League grounds of Lincoln City, Grimsby Town, Scunthorpe United, Boston United and Gainsborough Trinity, through the pyramid to some delightful local club grounds. Lavishly illustrated throughout with basic ground and club information for fans and groundhoppers alike.

Available from Amazon – August 2022

The Mont

– 125 years of the Mexborough Montagu Hospital Charity Cup 1897-2022

FA Cup winners, World Cup players and some of the game's greatest names have played in 'The Mont' – a charity competition that has defied the years in the heart of South Yorkshire.

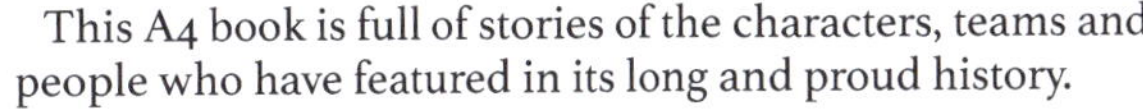

This A4 book is full of stories of the characters, teams and people who have featured in its long and proud history.

Available as a paperback – December 2022
www.montagucup.com/order-mont-postage

PENNY
for your
SPORTS
ONE PENNY
1964

Printed in Poland
by Amazon Fulfillment
Poland Sp. z o.o., Wrocław